Our Family Genealogy: the Pickens Family

Wanda Austin Nelson

Disclaimer:
This book is intended only for family history preservation. The author is not claiming any of this research to be solely her own. It is not intended to be for any historical documentation. It is only for preserving family records. Neither the author nor the publisher shall be held liable or responsible to any person or entity, directly or indirectly, for any information in this book. All the information therein has been documented by other researchers, including all the Pickens Family researchers. This book is to be used for general genealogy research, and to help record the data that many others have put together through long years of research. The author does not intend to infringe upon any of the work of others; this book is intended only to be a written record.

Credits:

Every Pickens family researcher, past and present, who have ever helped the author, or anyone, in any way.

Chapter One

In the Pickens Story, according to his website, Stuart C. Pickens (http://scpickens.tripod.com/pickens.html) states that "About 870 A.D. the Viking "Stirgud the Stout" and his men landed in the Orkneys and Northern Scotland. They came from Norway in an effort to expand. The Pickens name comes from this group of Vikings."

He continues, "Later, under their Earl, Thorfinn Rollo, they invaded France about 910 AD. They held Paris under siege until the French King, Charles the Simple, conceded defeat and granted Northern France to Rollo, who became the first Duke of Normandy."

"A descendant of Duke Rollo was Duke William who invaded England in 1066. William had a census taken in England in 1086 and compiled the Domesday Book. This Listing of names has Picken listed and many variations of the spelling as well. Most notably "Pinkeny" which in the 1200's lived in Picquigny in the Somme in the arrondisement of Amiens in Normandy."

William Picon is the earliest ancestor that we can identify. He was born circa 1520-1540, probably in France. He died at sea in 1567.

He was married to Ann Maria. His son was Robert Picon, born 1560 in La Rochelle, Manche, Basse-Normandie, France. Robert died in Midlothian, Scotland in the year 1644.

During the late 1500's, one Robert Picken/Picon from Scotland went to France during the reign of King Henry IV (1589 - 1610). He held a diplomatic post in the Kings Court until 1610 when Louis XIII took the crown. He then returned to Scotland near the English border and lived there until his death. He had family in Edinburgh, Stewarton, Glasgow, and the Kintyre Peninsula.

The border had become a friendly place at the time because a Scottish King sat on the English throne.

James I was also James VI of Scotland and the son of Mary, Queen of Scots. This made for what Robert thought would be an easy retirement.

It has been stated that Robert Picon had every inducement to stay in France and to convert to Catholicism. It has been inferred that by doing so, he would be able to keep his position in the French Court. By standing on his beliefs, and taking his family back to Scotland, he had to have known the danger and desperation of Scottish Presbyterians and other Protestants.

The years between 1680-1688 are known as the "Killing Time" because Charles II and James II slaughtered so many Presbyterians, and other Protestants, who refused to renounce their faith. Others faced prison, torture, and banishment. Robert Picon knew this, but he chose to stay true to his faith.

When his son Andrew was born in 1624, the political climate was getting difficult. King Charles I began his reign over England in 1625 and some of the attitudes changed toward the "Wily Border Reivers of Scotland", so called because of the old hatred between the two countries under Elizabeth I (1558 - 1603). The Covenanters were also uprising against the English crown and England's religious civil war was reaching into Scotland. The Scottish King James was no longer king and old hatreds built up again atop new hatreds.

It was still a tolerable life for Robert Picken/Picon, though, because of his diplomatic status. Robert Senior died in 1644 and is buried in Lowland Scotland.

The French Huguenots in the mid 1500's felt the same as the Scottish about religious persecution.

This common belief of religious freedom forged a friendship between the Scots and the French that lasted until 1685.

But, in those years, when Robert returned to Scotland, many were leaving Scotland to go to Ulster, Ireland and even to the New World.

The Picon's joined the tide of immigrants to Ireland. Persecution did not end there, though. By 1713, many dissenters of Catholicism were leaving Ireland and Scotland for the New World.

The Border Reivers were a strong force to be reckoned with, as well. The Picken family were among those who lived near the Scotland/England border.

The story of the Reivers dates from the 14th century and continued through into the late 17th century. It concerns the border between the two countries of England and Scotland. In those days, this Border displayed all of the characteristics of a frontier, lacking law, and order. Cattle rustling, feuding, murder, arson, and pillaging were all quite common occurrences.

A time when people owed their tribal or clan loyalty to their blood relatives or families. It was common for these families to straddle the Border.

The Reivers were just the one of the results of the constant English-Scottish wars that often reduced the Border area to a wasteland. The continued threat of renewed conflict offered little hope to productive farming. Why bother planting crops if they may be burned before they could be harvested? The reiving (raiding or plundering) of livestock was however a totally different matter, and so it became the principal business of the Border families.

The Reiver came from every social class from laborer to peer of the realm. He was your neighbor, your kinsman. He could be anyone.

He was a skilled horseman and fine guerrilla soldier, practiced in the fine arts of arson, kidnapping and extortion. There was no social stigma attached to reiving, it was simply an accepted way of life.

In 1703, a law was passed that required any office holder in Ireland to accept the sacraments of the Church of England. Although the Catholic Church was recognized as a legitimate religion, the Presbyterian faith had no legal recognition. Ministers were banned from their pulpits, prohibited to preach, to marry or even to bury parishioners. Teaching their faith was forbidden. The alienation of the Ulster Scots was profound.

Life in Ireland gradually became unjustifiable. Years of drought had devastated the economy, wiping out businesses and farmers. The land the Ulster Scots had settled on belonged to the Anglican English and Irish landlords. The farmers had to pay rent to the "lairds" who invariably raised rents in bad times as well as good. The final insult to the dedicated Presbyterians was the legal obligation to tithe to despised Church of England.

Drought was the final straw. Beginning in 1717 and lasting until 1775, five separate surges of emigration carried Ulster Scots to the shores of the American colonies.

The arrivals who emigrated between 1740-41 left Ireland to escape a famine that had killed almost 40,000 of their countrymen. These emigrants, specifically, were the people who arrived in Pennsylvania, and kept moving through the Valley of Virginia into the western borders of Virginia and then into the Carolinas. In all, by the early 1780's, two hundred and fifty thousand Ulster Scots had crossed the Atlantic Ocean to America.

They came in family groups and even individually. In several cases, entire congregations travelled together.

Chapter Two

Our line continues with Robert's son, William Andre (Andrew) Picon, born around 1624, in Edinburgh, Mid Lothian, Scotland. He died in Donegal, Donegal, Ireland, about 1655.

William Andre (Andrew) Picon married Isobel Matthinsone.

Robert Andre' (Andrew) I Picon was born about 1654, in Scotland. He went with his father to France, at a young age. There, he met and married a young widow named Esther Jeanne Benoit Bonneau, of La Rochelle, France. She was from a Protestant Huguenot family.

They began their family there in France. The families enjoyed a peaceful existence in France until 1685 when they revoked the Edict of Nantes. There was no more religious freedom in France unless you were Catholic. This was a good reason for Andrew and his family to return to Scotland and find their relatives. Robert and Esther, with his parents and his children, and a host of French friends, all went to Scotland to practice the Presbyterian faith.

William Henry Pickens was one of the sons of Robert Andrew Picon, born about 1669, in France.

He went to Ireland with his father by way of Campbelltown, Scotland. Several of the Pickenses went to the faraway tip of the Kintyre Peninsula to escape the strife and farm new land. It was 140 miles to the nearest city (Glasgow) along a thin strip of land, and it was only 14 miles across the water to Ireland (Ulster). Eventually Campbelltown became a busy port for refugees.

William Henry Pickens married Margaret Pike, the daughter of Gabriel Pike, of Ireland. William and Margaret had a total of nine children, all born in Ireland.

Israel born 1693; Margaret born 1695; Andrew born 1699; Robert Pike born 1697; William born 1705; John born 1710; Israel born 1712; Gabriel born 1715; and Lucy born 1718.

Once they came to America, the family added the final S onto their name and were known as Pickens.

By 1719, they were in America. They all appeared in Bensalem Church in Bucks County Pennsylvania as recent Immigrants from Ireland.

William Henry Pickens was elected Elder of the Dutch Reformed Church.

Israel Pickens married Martha Ann Davis, also from Ireland, about 1726. They married in Bucks County Pennsylvania.

Martha Ann was the daughter of George and Sarah Davis, and a sister of Nancy Ann, who married Andrew Pickens.

Martha Ann and Israel had six children. Two (Ann and William) were born in Bucks County Pennsylvania and the others were born after the family had moved to Virginia.

Ann was born in 1727, followed by William in 1728. Samuel was born 28 Apr 1743, the first of their children born in Virginia. Margaret was born about 1745, with Rebecca following in 1747. Hannah was the last child born to Israel and Martha Ann. Hannah was born in 1749.

Israel died in 1749, and his wife moved with their children to North Carolina.

William married Nancy Craig, daughter of John and Mary Elizabeth Blackwood Craig.

Mary Elizabeth Blackwood and her husband were both related to the noted Reverend John Craig, who pastored the Tinkling Spring Presbyterian Church of Augusta, Virginia for many years.

Church services in those days lasted all day, with breaks for the mid-day meal. It was a social gathering as much as worship service.

They had four children: Mary was born in 1768 and Margaret in 1773. Alexander followed in 1774, then Samuel in 1776.

In 1809, Alexander married Margaret McLarty, the daughter of Archibald McLarty, from Kintyre, Scotland.

Alexander and Margaret had eight children, seven were born in Cabarrus, North Carolina.

Martha Pickens was born in 1795, then William McKinney Pickens was born in 1813, followed by Archibald M. Pickens in 1815. Samuel Alexander Pickens was born in 1816 and Cyrus Pickens was born in 1817. John Allison Pickens was born in 1818 and Nancy Pickens about 1819.

The family relocated to Bedford, Tennessee where their last daughter was born, Margaret Jane Pickens in 1823.

In 1839 the family moved to Tishomingo County, Mississippi. They became members of the New Hope Presbyterian Church at Biggersville, Mississippi.

Archibald M. Pickens became a Presbyterian Minister and, in 1839, married Sarah Garrison, daughter of Samuel and Martha Morrison Garrison.

Archibald and Sarah made their home in the Bedford/Henderson, Tennessee area. They had eight children together.

Martha Virginia Pickens was born in 1839. She married William Lafayette Yancey from Fayette, Tennessee. They later moved to Clay County Arkansas, near William's cousin, Howard Jefferson Yancey.

Henrietta Pickens was born in 1841 and Euphenia Willie Pickens in 1842. Euphenia married S. J. Utley.

Cordelia "Delia" C. Pickens was born in 1843, and James Pickens in 1845.

Samuel Wing Pickens was born in 1847 and married Tennessee Brown.

Sarah Pickens was born in 1849. Cyrus A Pickens (named for his uncle) was born in 1853.

Chapter Three

Cyrus also went to Arkansas, and married a young widow, Abagail "Abby" Gill Stares Smith. Abby was the daughter of William and Kizzie Forrester Stares.

Cyrus and Abby were married on 19 May 1880, in Greene County, Arkansas, near his sister, Martha Virginia Pickens Yancey.

The photo is Cyrus and Abby with their daughters, Kizzie Ida (May) (seated), Julie and Virgie, and one of their sons, Albert. The young girl is their granddaughter, Pearl Yancey (leaning against her mother, Kizzie).

Cyrus and Abby Pickens had seven children. Albert was born 25 Sep 1886, William B, was born in 1887. Samuel A. was born in 1888 and Kizzie Ida (May) was born Dec 1891. John E. was born Aug 1894 and Delia Virginia was born 12 Nov 1896. Julia M. was born 02 Dec 1899.

Albert Pickens married Gertrude Effie Lehman and the lived in Los Angeles, California. He died 19 Feb 1956.

William Pickens died when he was only 17, on 05 Apr 1905.

Samuel Pickens died 20 Oct 1916 when he was 27.

Kizzie Pickens married J. H Jones when she was 06 Dec 1908 when she was 17. A few years later, on 14 Sep 1911, she married a widower, William Stephen Yancey. Will was a cousin of Cyrus' brother in law, William Lafayette Yancey.

John E. Pickens died 22 Nov 1914 at age 20.

Delia Virginia Pickens married Dallas Ebert Dorris and they relocated to Illinois, where she died in 1972.

Julia M. Pickens married Clarence Henry Payne in 1925. He was previously married to Lilly Slaughter.

Cyrus died about 1904, because Abby was married to Arthur F. Dollar by 1904. Arthur died in 1911, and Abby married John Charles Edwards in 1913. He died in 1916, and Abby never married again. She lived with her daughter, Julie, at the time of her death, in 1942.

Kizzie Pickens and Will Yancey only had one child, Pearl Evaline Yancey, born 18 Nov 1912.

Pearl married George Edward "Edd" Austin on 22 Sep 1928. They had nine children together, only three lived to be adults.

Pearl died 21 Aug 1941 of tuberculosis. Her three living children were all under the age of twelve.

Her oldest was barely eleven and his younger sisters were five and one.

Pearl:

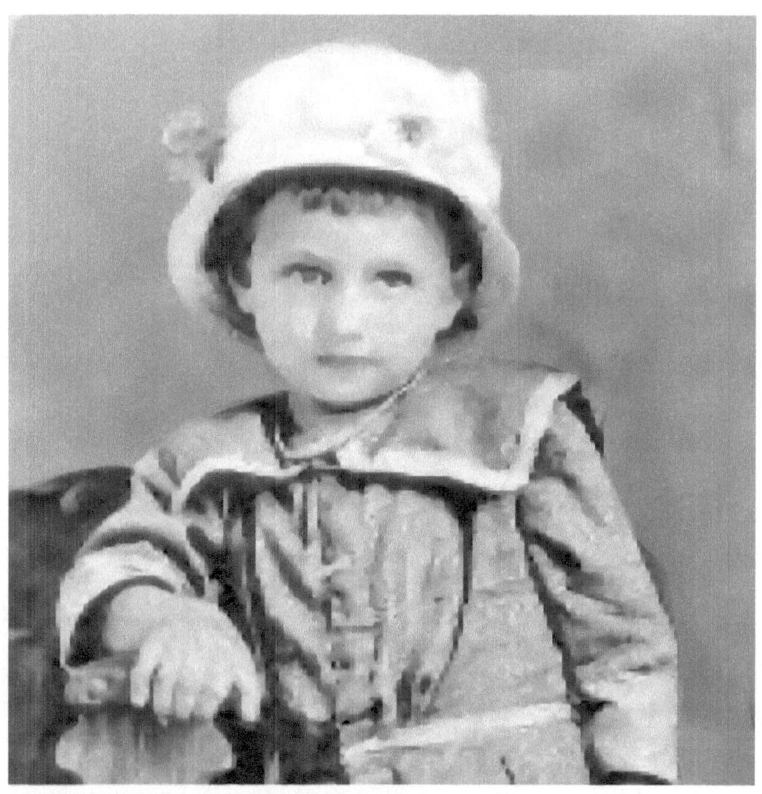

Chapter Four

Going back to the family of William Henry Pickens and Margaret Pike, of Bucks   Pennsylvania. Their youngest son was Gabriel, born in 1715.

Gabriel Pickens married Zerubiah Smith in 1742. He died about 1778 and Zerubiah moved to Tennessee with their son, Jonathon Pickens.

Jonathon was born in Abbeville, South Carolina, 1750. He married Mary Hogg and they had two sons, Gabriel and Jonathon Pickens, Jr.

Jonathon Pickens, Sr, died in 1830 at Hardin, Tennessee.

Gabriel Pickens was born in 1770 and married Mary Smith.

Jonathon Pickens, Jr, was born in 1775 and married Lydia Harrison. After Jonathon's death in 1825, Lydia remarried William Everett Rogers.

Jonathon and Lydia became parents to Hannah, born in 1783.

Hannah married Archibald Buchanan Davis in 1812. After living in Tennessee, they moved to Tishomingo, Mississippi where they lived until their deaths.

Archibald Davis was a descendant through his paternal line, to the Powhatan Indian family. He was a distant nephew of Pocahontas.

Hannah and Archibald Davis:

Lewis Pickens Davis was born in 1813 to Hannah and Archibald. John Lewis Davis followed in 1815.

Lewis Pickens Davis married Sarah Ann Ragsdale in 1849 at Alcorn County, Mississippi. She was the daughter of Abel and Nancy Axie Stanley Ragsdale.

Their daughter was A Mahala Davis, born 1850 in Mississippi.

A Mahala Davis married a blacksmith, Hugh Henry Henderson on 24 Apr 1867. Their son was John Henry Henderson, born 29 Aug 1873.

John Henderson also became a blacksmith and married Millie Jane Wren on 07 Jul 1895.

John and Millie had eight children: Mizzie Henderson, born 19 Oct 1897, Lillie May Henderson, born 08 Mar 1900, Alma Henderson, born 03 May 1903, Henry "Bud" Henderson, born 02 Mar 1906, Gertrue Henderson, born 21 Aug 1908, Alice Henderson, born 11 Feb 1910 (she died in 1913 of childhood diabetes), Ada Christen Henderson, born 08 Apr 1911 and Annie Ree Henderson, born 27 Jan 1920.

Mizzie married William Jasper Bragg on 15 Sep 1917 and they had five children. One of their daughters married the son of Pearl Yancey, the descendant of William Henry Pickens and Margaret Pike.

On the next page there is a photograph of Mizzie Henderson Bragg and Pearl Yancey Austin, the two descendants of Robert Picon.

Those two women never met each other but their children married and continued a merged line of the Pickens family.

Mizzie   Pearl

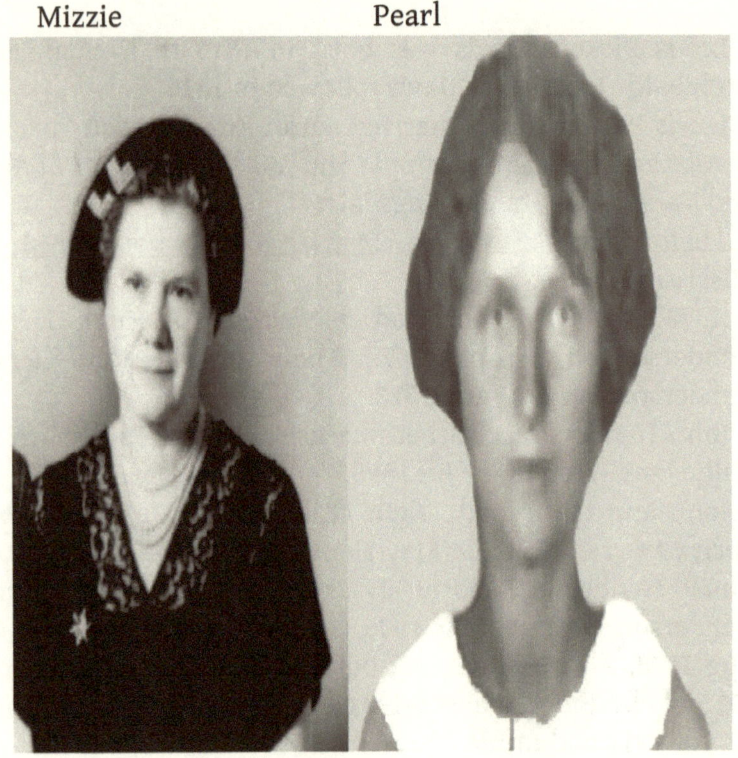

Wanda Austin Nelson has been a genealogist for over thirty years. This makes her tenth genealogy book in the series: Our Family Genealogy. She has also written some historical fiction as well as Christian inspirational.

She currently lives in Indiana but her favorite place is somewhere in the faraway mountains with a waterfall or a brook nearby. She would invite you over for coffee if you wanted to chat about genealogy!

All of her books are on Amazon. You can email her at: WandaNelson.Author@gmail.com

*On the following pages, there is plenty of room for you, the reader, to add any of your own research notes if you would like to.

Reader Notes:

www.ingramcontent.com/pod-product-compliance
Lightning Source LLC
Chambersburg PA
CBHW051145250726
48655CB00007B/3251